Words of Praise

"I cannot change yesterday. But I can impact today and the future. No matter what stage of life you find yourself in, it is never too late to start incorporating these principles. This book is already bearing fruit and helping us to be better parents and grandparents."

— Mark & Joy —

(Parents of Andrew, Abby, and Joshua)

"This book has helped us as parents to follow simple steps to raise our children to be humble and respectable people. It is very easy to read and apply to everyday life. There were many parts of the book that stood out to us and made us think "wow, we need to apply this to our parenting methods." We have children of all ages and each one of them are in different stages. This book has equipped us to be better parents and also enjoy our time with our children."

— Lee & Sara —

(Parents to Marlee, Cora, Claire, and Monroe)

Parenting
Through the Stages

Ron Olson & Reid Vander Veen

Parenting
Through the Stages

The Stages Parents Experience in their Relationships with their Children

Softcover ISBN: 978-1-7344127-4-1
Ebook ISBN: 978-1-7344127-5-8

Printed in the United States of America.

Cover and Layout Design: Amy Gehling
Editor: Dirk Lammers

www.theparentingmodel.com
Worthing, SD 57077

For my children - Lauren, Olivia, Regan, Levi, and Kylen,

Your dad is very proud of each of you. Being your father brought me incredible joy.

— I love you. Jesus bless you —

For my grandkids – Finley, Ronan, Ezra, Auden, Willa, Revel,

and the many more to come

I've cherished every moment with each of you and I love being

— Your Grandpa —

For Renee,

"Thank you for being the mother of my children and believing in me. I'm so glad I'm married to you. I love you."

— Ron —

For Ronan, Auden, and Revel,

Daddy loves you very, very much.

For my parents – Ron and Sheri Vander Veen

Thank you for modeling a loving, selfless relationship for me and the kids. We cannot thank you enough for all that you do for us.

For Lauren,

I'm so thankful our children have you as their mommy. You are an incredible woman. Marrying you is the best decision I've ever made. I love you.

— Reid —

To Luke Smith,

Thank you for helping to capture and articulate much of what's been included in the following pages. Your friendship and discipleship are cherished gifts to both witness and experience first-hand.

To Ron,

My heart aches knowing you won't ever hold a finished copy of this book in your hands. Yet, I smile knowing you had little interest in the book itself, only what it could do, what it would mean. Your only desire was to impact lives in a positive way. I'm honored that you trusted me to help you accomplish that dream.

Your life touched so many. And your legacy is one that will live on and continue to do so. We thank you for inspiring, teaching, and leading us all.

No words can describe how much you're missed.

I love you, Ron.

— Reid —

Table of Contents

Foreword

It started as a passing comment. "We should write a book about that," I said to my father-in-law as he described his model for parental relationships. It was probably the fourth or fifth time I'd heard it. Ron always knew when he had good material. Whether it was a story from his past or an original thought, if he was sure about it, then you could be sure you'd hear about it. And probably more than once.

Ron was never short on theory. A farmer his entire life, he spent many quiet moments alone in a tractor or semi, in the shop, or in the field. It offered a great deal of time to think. As a man who loved family and relationships more than anything on this earth, Ron was a regular listener of talk radio about families and parenting. Over the years he'd compiled what he'd heard and read and boiled down his own beliefs into a simple framework for parenting. The five-step model discussed in the following pages is that framework.

But theory alone isn't enough. Theories must be applied in order to prove their value. As it happens, Ron and Renee have five kids. Raising five children on a farm in South Dakota might not seem like your picture of perfection, but it was Heaven on Earth for Ron. Renee and a few of the kids might even agree on the right day. If nothing else, it offered a beautiful testing ground to prove out and polish off the ideas found in the following pages.

When the idea for this book came together, it was hard not to chuckle at the concept. Even for us. On one hand you had a guy whose comfort level with a computer was mostly checking auction sites and eBay listings, and pecked at the keyboard with his pointer fingers on both hands. On the other hand, you had a guy who was a novice writer with no kids. And together they decided to write a book on parenting. I have a lot of favorite stories about Ron, but that will forever be one of them. My willingness, and even desire at times, to do something unconventional was only ever matched by Ron's. His eagerness and enthusiasm to do things that others might consider unusual, bizarre, or avant-garde made him one of my favorite people to be around.

Ron's life came to an abrupt and early end in January of 2020. He and Renee were on their way to meet with their community group at church when an oncoming vehicle crossed the centerline and the two vehicles collided. Renee has since made a full recovery. Ron, however, passed away on the scene. He was 56.

We'd only recently received the edited manuscript of this text. Ron hadn't yet read it.

He was one of my favorite people in the whole world. A mentor, a teacher, a business partner, a father, a grandfather, and a friend.

What follows is a simple model that explains the relationship dynamics between parents and children at various stages of development, from discipline at an early age all the way through friendship as adults. Whether you had a fantastic upbringing or one that was less than ideal, this book is for you. It offers a simple framework to follow as you consider the uniqueness of your children and how your role changes as a parent as they grow and mature. The result is a fantastic friendship and your children operating as functional, contributing adults, hopefully willing to repeat the process all over again with your grandchildren.

Introduction

Few people who have parented would call the role "easy." Parents face new challenges every day as our children grow, learn, and change seemingly by the minute. Because of that, our parent-child relationships can be quite complex, but they don't have to be.

In this book, we explore a simple model that you, as parents, can use and adapt to your relationship with each of your children. We identify five stages that we all progress through in our parent-child relationships, and each stage carries significant importance. Within each stage we find key lessons that we must instill and observe in our children before we progress to the next stage. The order of these stages is of utmost importance, so we encourage you to stick to the particular sequence outlined in this book.

We believe you'll find value in this five-stage model whether you're a first-time expecting parent or the mother or father of four. And each of your children will be benefit from your investment in this approach. We're confident that if you read this book and put into practice the teachings found inside, you'll be in a better place as a parent, have a stronger relationship with each of your children, and develop an understanding and appreciation for the ultimate destination in your parent-child relationship.

Our model is simple, but that does not mean it's easy. Many of us have learned from models that would not line up with the one explained in this book, and some readers may have been raised with no model at all. Others may come from a background of incredibly poor examples set by the adults and parents in our lives. By no fault of your own, you may lack a proper example or model that you can follow as you raise and develop a relationship with your own children. Some readers may come from a wonderful home and have experienced a great relationship with their own parents throughout their lives. Even so, you may lack a simple, well-thought-out model to mimic and use as a guide as you set out on your own parenting adventure. Readers from all of these backgrounds should find great value in these lessons.

In the coming pages, we'll explain the five-stage model and dive into each in great detail, but please remember to follow the proper order. In as little as 45 minutes, you'll find a new understanding of the stages and progress through each with care and commitment to your children's future.

— CHAPTER ONE —

Discipline

What comes to mind when you think of the word discipline? For many of us, the word drums up a series of negative memories from our past. For Reid, the term brings back specific memories of youth in which he misbehaved and paid the price—those "Wait until your dad gets home" sort of moments.

Discipline is a form of corrective action resulting from undesired behavior. Most situations we encounter carry an understood code of behavior, and failure to comply with this code (misbehaving) requires corrective action (discipline.) When delivered well, discipline reminds us of an expected behavior while highlighting the disobedience and how expectations were not met. The explanation commonly carries a form of discipline or recourse as corrective action, which attempts to prevent the misbehavior from reoccurring while instilling new lessons.

One thing we've learned as we've studied discipline is that appropriate discipline leads to security. And if we could identify things we want for our children at a young age, most of us would likely rank security near the top of the list. To establish an environment of security, we first need to set clear boundaries and codes of expected behavior for our children and our families. Those codes of behavior must be created and maintained with high consistency.

Here's a common example: You instruct your child not to touch the hot burner on top of the stove. You've set a clear code of behavior for your little one and made well-known the expected behavior and boundaries. Yet, your defiant child touches it anyway, perhaps out of curiosity. The logic coursing through that beautiful little brain has not yet fully understood that every behavior, both good and bad, brings with it some sort of outcome or consequence. Figuring they can touch the stove quickly while your back is turned to avoid detection, your little one reaches for the stove and immediately cries out in pain. "Duh," you think to yourself. "I told you not to touch that."

Unfortunately, there's something missing inside that little brain that prevents your child from truly understanding your instruction. Despite our best efforts to explain to our children why they shouldn't touch a hot stove, the logic required to adequately understand both the instruction and the consequences of defiant behavior simply aren't present in minds that young. The codes of behavior we've created, though simple and straightforward to us, can be too complex for our little ones to understand. There's a very negative (and painful) consequence to that behavior, and it's not simply disappointing Mom or Dad. Unfortunately, up to this point in their lives, that disappointment may be the only consequence our child has come to understand, and thus the pain is a new type of consequence. Even if the instruction included some reference to the amount of heat or pain that they might experience, the undeveloped brain has a difficult time linking cause and effect—that is, until the hand blisters with pain.

Let's take a minute to try to understand what's going on in the mind of our little one in this example. Due to the age and stage of development, your son or daughter only possesses the very basics of understanding logic. Even with proper explanation, the logic you're trying to instill into your young child's brain may be slightly more complex than he or she can handle. Although obvious to us, the amount of information required to process and compute this situation adequately can prove difficult for our little ones.

In the hot stove scenario, we parents try to explain a natural cause-and-effect relationship. It's easy for us to understand, but our basis for understanding comes from a lifetime of experience with other cause-and-effect situations. We've experienced pain and have developed a good sense as to the source of that pain and how to avoid it. We've misbehaved ourselves and paid the price a time or two. The idea is not profound, but that doesn't mean it will necessarily prove easy to articulate in a way an 18-month old might understand. Try as we may, it will be difficult for Timmy or Suzy to logically process the likely outcome of such behavior because of their significantly smaller frame of reference. They are able to comprehend only small amounts of discipline and logic. As we begin to dive into our parent-child relationship model, we'll start by taking advantage of this wonderful and exciting time in the lives of our children to help them learn quickly and make our lives as parents much easier.

New Sources of punishment

Why did our little one touch the stove even though we specifically told them not to? One of the things many parents forget is that at this stage, we've been protecting our children at such a high level that consequences or punishment typically only come from us. Our disappointment as parents may have been the only real source of consequences they've ever faced. If they're lucky, we may have already involved other caring adults, but their experience with discipline would still be limited to disappointing the adults or caretakers in their lives. Because we love and care for our children, they of course express sadness when they know they've disappointed us, but their hyperactive minds and imaginations combined with limited life experience makes that sad feeling quickly disappear. It doesn't help when some parents immediately follow any sort of scolding or corrective language with a hug or a treat—talk about a confusing message for our kids. We must realize that the only logic coursing through our child's beautiful little brain is the thought that, "I will only experience a negative outcome if Mom catches me in the act. Without that, there's nothing to worry about." Unfortunately for the child, Mom and Dad will not always be the only source of consequences in their lives, and this stove-top scenario is a common first lesson for many children.

At this stage we have likely not yet been able to instill into our children the value of thinking through these problems on their own and understanding them at a deeper level. That's not because we haven't tried. It's because the early development of the brain hasn't made sense of these complicated thought procedures.

So, what should we do?

One of the first things we must do in this initial stage is to build up a system in the child's brain that isn't focused solely on "me," "mine," and "I want, I want, I want." It may sound extreme, but at some level this involves removal of the child's self-centered, selfish ways. We must get rid of the portion of that child's old self that is solely focused on their own desires. This by no means suggests that we want to eliminate or modify the personality or the identity of the child. Rather, we must get rid of the self-centeredness and begin to create a code of behavior that doesn't revolve around the child's personal desires. We must eliminate the notion that any time they whine or cry they will get what they want. We must get rid of the "me," "mine," "I win" attitudes of our children. Every subsequent stage is filling back up with new self, new education, and new information, and all of these eventually lead to the complete fulfillment of the child. But we must start by breaking down their selfish understanding of the world, and the earlier the better. It may seem intense to begin this level of discipline with a newborn, infant, or toddler, but we assure you, the earlier you begin this stage, the easier it will be.

Don't think that just because you're the parent you won't be learning, growing, and challenging yourself through this process, too. This initial step is a big one. When will you start this process? How soon will you be willing to make the required commitment to your children? The sooner, the better. If you think you're ready, let's dive in.

Breakdown, rebuild

We begin with a profound yet simple concept. We must quickly and carefully break down the will of our children. However, we must do this without breaking the child's spirit. This is perhaps the most crucial point that will be made in this book. Break down the will, but not the spirit. It's a model used by many in the military during early stages of training. We break down the will of the children, but we do not leave them there. Done well, discipline is only as good as the follow-up. If you abandon them after breaking down their will, you're left simply with a broken-down child. Like building muscle through working out, we break them down so they can be built back up bigger, better, and stronger. We do this so they can grow back more complete than before.

This parenting model is a five-course meal, and discipline is the appetizer. This is the beginning, and for many it's the most difficult part of the process. The idea of using military training techniques on our beautiful little babies may be a hard concept for some to grasp, but we can do this in a delicate way. You don't have to be a drill sergeant daddy or Marine Corps mommy every day, but these concepts are sound.

All forms of discipline enforcement come down to two simple ideas: corporal punishment and separation. Now, before you go throw a fit or write emails explaining other forms of discipline, let us explain: It's our belief that throughout life, even as adults, we experience all discipline in one of these two forms.

There will be moments while raising our children in which force is required. This may come in the form of picking them up and removing them from a situation. It may come from a corrective flick of the ear to stop fidgeting. It may come from some sort of restraint so as to prevent harmful behavior. In our earlier example, it comes in the form of painful burn on the hand. These are common responses by parents that, when used wisely, can be valuable training and learning techniques for our children.

Consider the many forms of punishment that involve separation. We put the worst offenders in prison, and separate them from the freedoms most of us experience every day. Parents will at times ground a child, remove cell phone privileges, or take away a video game. These are all forms of separation, removing us from the things we desire. Get a speeding ticket? You'll be separated from your license and the ability to drive. Hit your sister with your toy hammer? No more toy hammer. Got it?

Corporal punishment as love

Reid was spanked as a child, and he thanks God that his parents had the courage and strength to help him understand the idea of action and consequence early on, and they did so in a way that made him only want to learn each lesson once.

We realize the risk taken here starting off a book discussing spanking and military-style training, especially in this day and age. And although many on both sides of the fence would argue the pros and cons of spanking children, let me take a quick minute to discuss why, at least from a conceptual level, it may make sense.

It may seem unfair or exaggerated for some of you to classify these types of corrective actions as corporal punishment, but it's true. For the sake of this book (and the well-being of your children) let's make sure not to take the ideas of physical punishment, or corporal punishment in this case, too lightly.

The trouble with corporal punishment is that, when done from any mental state other than love, it very quickly becomes abuse. As a parent, the second your mind is not in the right place while disciplining in this form, you are abusing that child. Now, that's not to scare you off from this form of discipline for your little ones. In fact, it's required. Remember, without this there's only one other form of discipline, separation, and separation alone carries with it a host of negative long-term consequences. The two forms must be used together.

Many parents struggle with disciplining children, and that trepidation often is rooted in their upbringing. Some parents struggle with showing any emotion at all. We must resist the temptation to bottle up our emotions and disappointments when our children misbehave. We must also resist the desire to be quick to make excuses for poor behavior. One of the worst things we can do as a parent is make excuses for our children when they do wrong. "Oh, it was just that one time," or "He didn't actually mean to hit that other boy," provide examples of a parent doing far more harm than good to their children. We need to remember our role as parents. We need to hold ourselves and our children to a higher standard of behavior.

Clinical Psychologist and Author Dr. Jordan B Peterson says it this way in his book *12 Rules for Life: An Antidote to Chaos:* "Do not let your children do anything that makes you dislike them." That's not easy. People can be mean, even adults—especially adults. The only way to prevent mean adults is to appropriately and lovingly correct mean and misbehaving children. And it must start at a very early age.

This attitude and approach also brings with it a few major concerns, the most significant of which is that when we finally take a step to start disciplining, it's often too late. That can quickly result in an attempt to discipline out of a place of anger rather than love. We urge you not to be the type that waits to react until you reach a boiling point and can't take it anymore. A quote we love from Lt. David Marquet's book *Turn the Ship Around* suggests that, "A little rudder far from rocks is better than a lot of rudder near the rocks." Adjustments are much easier made in small increments over time.

Let's take a look at a few different forms of our two types of discipline on the following page.

Corporal punishment:

- Swatting of the hand: "Don't touch that. It's hot!"
- Spanking
- Flicking of the ear: "Don't sleep in class or church."
- Pinching: "Quit acting like a toddler."
- Conditioning: "If you're not going to practice hard or take this seriously, we'll run sprints."

Separation:

- Curfew: "You may not stay out late with your friends."
- Grounding: "You may not be with your friends at all."
- Denial of desires: "You will not get that toy or snack because you're acting like a toddler."
- Time out: "If you cannot play nice, then you won't be allowed to play at all."
- Taking away of rights: "You lose your cell phone for a week since you're using too much data, or not paying attention in class, or texting inappropriate or mean things."
- No dessert: "If you won't eat your peas, you don't get ice cream."
- Benching: "You're not allowed to play this game because you didn't attend practice."

Or worse:

- You don't get to attend the college of your choice because you didn't study.
- You get jail time because you broke the law. You are removed from public and your freedoms are withheld.

Logic progression - Further explanation of the concept

Corporal punishment is often the most effective form of discipline when we're at a stage in our child's development that he or she possesses very little or no logic of their own. The logic progression of young children goes something like this: They hold no logic of their own, then they rely on the parent's logic as they develop it for themselves, then they develop a near complete logical capability on their own. In the early stage, the child likely does not possess the capability to process a string of thoughts and understand complex logic or reasoning. Think back to the hot-stove example. Also, how many of you have you ever tried to have an adult conversation using reason and logic with a toddler in a toy store or a grandchild at the grocery store? How'd that work out for you?

We must simplify our message. This is a good reminder whether we have kids or not, but it's particularly important with children.

The ultimate goal in the discipline stage is compliance—compliance without questioning. Children in this phase of our model are unable to think long-term or see the wide-angle picture in every situation. When done correctly, appropriate discipline allows you to skip the process that involves your child attempting to reason with themselves on whether or not to follow the will of the parent. This is absolutely crucial when our children are young.

Think of a child running into a busy street—maybe your child. Parents need to be able to stop that child without hesitation. We need to have discipline so instilled in that child that when we yell, "Stop!" we know with certainty that our child will immediately and without hesitation listen and follow our command. We do not have the luxury of that child considering any alternative behaviors in that scenario. You do not want to have to wonder whether they will comply, nor do you want to have to explain why they need to listen. At that very moment, 100-percent compliance is absolutely vital to the safety of that child.

Upon that child being back in a safe environment, we can then take advantage of the teaching moment. We can begin to discuss with them the reasons why they cannot run into the busy street, authoring on their behalf the first strings of logic they can begin to rely on for themselves in the future. In the beginning, we must use very simple if/then statements as a model for the development of that logic. But standing in the middle of the road with oncoming traffic is not the time for them to sit and ponder. Complete, unquestioning compliance is the only acceptable action.

Logic progression: Stage 1 - No logic

The beauty of your child having zero or very little reasoning capability of their own is that we can capitalize on the opportunity and very quickly instill this concept of discipline. Discipline is the foundation for the entire relationship between parents and children, and it is also one of the greatest gifts we can provide for our children as they mature and enter adulthood. We've all seen helicopter parents, and have likely poked fun at them or commented as to how we'll never be like that. If you don't want to be a helicopter parent, if you don't want to straddle your kids until they're teenagers, you need to start with discipline and compliance. You don't need to be perfect, but you do need to be confident and consistent.

How many of you have been at a dinner party with family friends and have observed the one child or group of siblings who dominate the festivities. Children push the boundaries of what is allowed by seeking attention through temper tantrums, stealing toys, or not eating politely at the table. The only reason this happens is because of weak parenting. It is unlikely the child's fault that he or she is behaving this way. We've trained them to do so, whether we care to admit it or not. Every time they act out, we give them attention. In their minds, this reinforces the idea that, "When I want Mom's attention, or when I feel Dad is ignoring me, start to behave like a brat and they'll focus on me." This is particularly dangerous when parents are too weak to discipline at a level that will correctly alter that child's behavior.

The little terrorist in the living room is not going to magically change his behavior by a stern glare or a, "Now, Timothy, play nice," sort of comment. If history has proven anything by this point it's that these tactics do not work on your child, and you are too weak or too focused on saving face in front of your friends to properly discipline. Believe me, you're not helping your cause. Everyone there is annoyed by your lack of action, not Timothy's behavior.

Discipline at its most basic level is about correcting poor behavior. However, the other side to that coin, and an area where many parents also struggle, is rewarding positive behavior. These two simple tasks—celebrating the little wins and rewarding positive behavior while correcting or adjusting for negative behavior—quickly begin to hardwire our children as to what is and what is not appropriate.

This is why disciplining at an early age is much easier than many would think. Parents often mistakenly believe that in order to discipline their child, the child must possess the ability to logic and reason. Parents believe they cannot discipline their child until there is some heightened level of computing power present in their little brains that would allow them to understand the why of discipline. This is nearly the equivalent of expecting our children to walk before we teach them to crawl. We must instill discipline before free will, free-thinking, and logic develop the ability to get in the way, not the other way around.

We do a sad disservice when we wait until our children develop reasoning abilities of their own. Children who are not disciplined early justify reasons not to comply with desires or commands of their parents and other authority figures. They do this because they are still incapable of seeing the full picture or any perspective other than their own simple, selfish viewpoint.

Why?

Ronan started asking, "Why?" around 2 years old. At every instruction, he'd ask, "Why?" 19 times before he was satisfied with the direction. This is a clear sign that logic is beginning to arrive. He has both the ability and the desire to compute at a higher level. We must begin instilling discipline before this happens. That's critical. Most children naturally enter this state of questioning, and there's a big difference between defiance and seeking clarity. Without establishing a foundation of discipline prior to this stage setting in, children may ask, "Why?" out of defiance rather than out of an effort to seek clarity and understanding. This is not their fault; it's ours. There is a sequence of order here that makes each of these stages easier. It's not impossible to correct if you are out of order, but it is significantly more difficult.

When we neglect to correct early, we fail to take advantage of those early years when our children are most pliable and most able to learn. At this stage, our children are growing rapidly (not that you needed the reminder.) Parents often wait until their children are 2-3 years old to begin making any attempt at discipline, and by that time, the child already has begun setting foundations for logic and reason based on other things, the least of which is respect for elders. We've failed to implant in their brain the idea that children must honor those in authority, at least not frequently enough that they'll remember. And we may have missed our best opportunity to provide them with the understanding that good behavior is rewarded and bad behavior is punished.

If you are not telling your child, "No," by the time he or she is 6 months old, you're doing it wrong. We don't care if they don't understand a word you're saying or can only speak in squeaks and screams, discipline starts at birth. By the time the average child is 1 year old, they should have the ability to fully grasp what it means when Mom or Dad (or anyone else) says, "No." I do not get that toy, I do not get to get out of bed, I do not get to touch that, eat that, or place it anywhere near my mouth.

Consistency is key during this programming phase. Imagine you're on the right track. You've done very well at disciplining little Suzy in the past and are making great progress—that is, right up until she throws a temper tantrum in the grocery store. (Yes, those will still happen.) If you quickly cave in to Suzy because you either don't have the patience, are on the tail end of a long day at work, or simply want to avoid embarrassment, you've suddenly crossed the wires for little Suzy. This new behavior and outcome sequence that she just experienced has instantly begun a reprogramming of sorts for her little brain. At a minimum, she's getting confusing signals about the types of responses she'll get for various behaviors. Initiate a stern, corrective, adult-like conversation with Suzy about why now is neither the right time nor place for this type of behavior and provide corrective action. After all, if we want our children to act like adults, we should treat them as such.

As parents we also need to make sure we're on the same page. We need to create clear expectations for desired behavior and the roles we will play. Done correctly, this will quickly continue down to our children. We will begin to set clear expectations to our children.

Leaving discipline

Perhaps the most important thing to remember is that we need to leave the discipline stage. Don't rush it, but we want to get through this stage as quickly as possible. We must also remember that a good portion of this stage is positive. Discipline brings many negative connotations and ideas, but it can be very positive. Think about yourself for a moment. If you consider yourself disciplined, that likely brings with it many happy thoughts. It may even generate a smile across your lips as you consider how you were disciplined enough recently to save and afford that vacation, or how you lost weight as part of your diet goals. These are all fantastically positive things that are the result of strong discipline! Why on earth would we want to withhold that ability and instruction from our children?

As parents, we ultimately need to release control. If all we provide is control, discipline may have a counterproductive result. Parents score all over the scale in terms of how well we provide this discipline. Some can be too hard on our children in this stage, and others too soft. This is why creating a child requires two people. We must be able to provide balance to one another for our children. This can be tough for single parents, as you'll need to play both roles. Better yet, find someone or a group of people that will support your efforts. If not this, then you'll need to find a nearly ideal balance between the two, which will prove quite difficult.

Our goal as parents is to enter this stage and process, get discipline to set in as quickly but as thoroughly as possible, and move on to the next stage. On its own, discipline can be detrimental. It needs to be done from a heart of love and from the perspective that we will continue to build on this in a positive manner in the next stages of the model. We need to ensure that we are working towards leaving this stage, not working hard to remain in it.

The ultimate goal is self-discipline, which is achieved when we no longer have to focus our efforts on disciplining our children and they begin to do it for themselves. We've slowly transitioned the baton of discipline over to the child, but we must first establish discipline. Parents' failure to establish discipline can be really hard on kids, especially when they have to grow up (and believe me, it will be a painful childhood for them and for you.) If our kids are forced to fight through these issues at 30 years old, or when they have their first child, they will find it to be an incredibly long, painful process. For the lucky ones, they may figure it out, though it won't be easy. For the others? The perpetual cycle of poorly behaved children and adults will continue.

Final exam

Discipline is the only stage for which there is a final exam, at least of sorts. Successful discipline is easy to notice. If you've ever owned a dog, you can probably quickly come up with a few examples of what discipline looks like. After a while of training, they realize that they get punished when they do their business in the house and get lots of love and attention, praise, and rewards for taking that business outside. They also know that if they obey commands like "Sit," "Stay," "Come here," "Lay down," and "Roll over," they often get rewarded. This is learned discipline in one of its simplest forms. Don't try to convince me that you can't get through to your kids when you can teach Fido the difference between a chew toy and antique furniture, or get him to sit still with that treat balancing on his nose until you give the command to eat it. Please have higher hopes for your children.

Here's a real-life example for those of us with two legs. Renee, Ron's wife, had a very simple goal when it came to the discipline stage and raising her five kids. She wanted the assurance that if she yelled "Stop!" all five of those kids would instantly stop moving, stop what they were doing, and freeze like statues. There are some very practical reasons for this. Heavy equipment, livestock, and chemicals present real danger when growing up on a farm. And on the roads nearby, a 20-foot-wide tractor or a pickup screaming by at 70 mph pose additional risks. For Renee, it was very simple. She needed to know with absolute certainty that she could prevent an accident if she felt she was about to see one.

This example of knowing your kids will behave according to your commands is a very simple test that the discipline stage offers. Even if you don't live on a farm, the same applies to kids playing near a busy city street or a suburban road with heavy traffic. The idea here is to find a test that is relevant for you and your family.

Think of anything you'd like your kids to do at the very moment you first tell them. It could be to get ready for bed, do their homework, or get into the shower. Whatever it is, parents can always issue a test command to see how they're doing on the discipline phase. Ultimately, these little tests will confirm for you that you've succeeded in establishing discipline into your child. The other side benefit of these little tests is that you can also use them as a gauge to see how your child is doing with respecting elders. The parent-child relationship is one thing, but this is especially true if you are not the one issuing the commands. If your sister, co-worker, the parent of your child's friend, or your child's coach asks or tells them to do something (or to stop doing something), your child's behavior in the moments immediately following provides a fantastic window into the status of their development through this stage.

We'd encourage you to give this a shot. Do it a couple times today. Do it a few times a week for all your children, regardless of the stage they may be in. As mentioned previously, discipline, once established, rarely leaves. We may call on discipline less, hopefully, as our kids progress through the process, but the foundation of discipline is one that can last a lifetime.

Let me issue a slight warning to go along with these little experiments in discipline. If your child fails, you must be prepared to hit the pause button on the later stages of the process and spend a bit more time back in the discipline phase.

Consistency is key

Parents must remain consistent with children of different ages and in different stages of this model, and we'll illustrate this point through some friends we'll call Jake and Theresa. Not so long ago, we were regularly getting together with a few other families at the home of Jake and Theresa, who have three beautiful daughters. Their oldest was 9, the next was 6, and the youngest was 1 year old. Being great parents, they worked toward beginning discipline training on the youngest at an early age; however, when she would disobey, they would often laugh it off and fail to enforce the disciplinary requests and commands. Now we understand that no one is perfect, but the trouble with Jake and Theresa behaving like this is that they would do so in front of their two older children. As parents, their stock quickly changed in the eyes of their older kids. This was obvious to those of us observing over the course of a few weeks. The two older children, too, quickly began to ignore commands, disobey their parents, and press their luck around the house. They had seen their parents on multiple occasions issue a command or make a request that was blatantly disregarded and there was absolutely no follow-through on punishment. The youngest child was running that whole house, whether any of them would dare to admit it.

This is a natural process for children. The only way to find a boundary is to regularly push towards the limits and eventually find them. Too often, there is a large difference between where we say a boundary exists and where we enforce one.

A classic example on the boundary-seeking side of things is a story of Regan, Ron and Renee's middle child, eating in the kitchen. The kids had clear and explicit instructions that they had to be in the kitchen while eating. Regan regularly committed to see how firm that boundary really was. As the story goes, she executed various little tests to determine exactly what it meant to be in the kitchen vs out of the kitchen. Such tests included standing with one foot on the kitchen floor and the other on the carpet of the other room, standing in the kitchen but hovering one foot over the line, etc.. The creative (and sometimes rebellious) one that she is, took it upon herself to find the very perimeter of her permissions.

And we can't forget about the follow through. If we threaten a punishment or some sort of specific disciplinary action, we must be willing to enforce it. Few stories highlight this as well as the time Ron was driving the kids around in his pickup and Levi was acting out. Levi was probably four or five years old in this instance. At one point during the drive Ron made the threat that if he didn't shape up and start behaving, he'd end up in the back of the truck. It wasn't long until Levi and his entire car seat were removed from the cab of the truck. Ron put the entire thing in the bed of the truck as they continued the drive. Levi was safely strapped into the car seat, but he slid around the box of that truck like a pinball for a few minutes before being allowed back into the cab. It remains undetermined if his attitude was improved because he was so scared or because he had so much fun. Either way, the threat was fulfilled and the rest of the drive was significantly more pleasant. All the kids experienced the benefit of understanding that when dad threatens a punishment, it's not just talk. This should highlight the importance of being precise in our speech and choosing our words, and threats, wisely. Especially when dealing with our kids.

The goal here is not to break kids of free-thinking or to prevent them from having the ability to make decisions. In fact, the opposite is actually true. Incorporating discipline prior to free-thinking is much easier on both parents and children. The earlier you incorporate discipline into the process, the easier it will be for your child to see the big picture. They will have a much greater ability to think through their decisions, consider the alternatives and achieve potential outcomes. Without the added discipline component, our children will continue to make impulse decisions based on whatever feels right without considering the long-term effects and consequences.

If discipline is successful, the instruction of it goes away. It dissipates. It's less needed. We must also remember that lessons of discipline will continue even as we progress through various stages of this model. It will change shape and solidify over time. If you can do the awkward or difficult things early on, your hardest work as a parent can be done by the time your child reaches age 4 or 5. From there, it's all building on the foundation that has been created and instilled in that child. No, their teenage years will not be free from issues, pain, and disappointment. Your child is human after all. But we'd be willing to wager they will be much easier to parent than someone who hasn't been instilled with discipline. It's the foundation and footing to your house. The crux of the issue is that if you're unwilling to discipline your child, you are not disciplined. If you look around and take an honest look at the situation and cannot find the issue, YOU very likely may be the issue. This stage is as much about being disciplined as a parent as it is about disciplining the child. The cycle starts or breaks down here. There is no more crucial point in the system.

— CHAPTER TWO —

Training

The training stage, or teaching stage, is the second step in our journey. We discussed in the previous chapter that discipline is often the hardest, but the rigidity and firmness of parents is equally crucial in this stage. We must help discipline continue to set in while avoiding new bad habits from forming as our children's skills and development progress. Fortunately, if you've been going through this process with your children from birth, they already likely possess a great deal more reasoning and understanding than they otherwise would have. This will help ease the process in this stage.

A word of caution: Stubbornness is common for many children. This is not an argument against the model, at this stage or any other; it's merely the child being a child and figuring out the ways of the world. This is an absolutely crucial period in their development, one that if handled properly can assist with putting that child on a great path to mature adulthood.

The transition to the training stage begins as soon as logic appears to be present. When a child or young person presents enough internal logic to process thoughts and provide reasoning, it is an indication that we can begin working into the training stage. This is true regardless of what those thoughts may be. We're not looking for our child to be the next Mozart. Even simple or completely random thoughts, as many will be at this age, indicate the ability for our transition to begin.

Many professionals who study the behavior of young children argue that most often they will possess the ability to know what to do in a given situation long before they know why they should be performing that behavior. A simple example of this would be the loud noises a child makes when at play or having fun. They may experience a feeling of fun and excitement without understanding why the sudden release of energy or burst of volume affects their mood or attitude. Similarly, when a young child at the table refuses to eat, many parents, us included, will offer up some sort of transaction to the young person. "If you eat two more bites, you can get down and go play." At some point, the child will begin to understand the nature of the offer and hopefully willingly participate. However, it will be much later before they understand that eating those few additional bites of green veggies is going to help them improve or maintain health. That level of logic is called upon down the road. For now, we want to take advantage of those initial glimpses of computing power present in our little ones' minds.

For many children entering this stage, a range of 12-18 months would be an estimation of when basic logic presents itself. Again, discipline overlaps, but when reasoning starts, training can begin to take place. At this stage, there is a very simple goal to keep in mind, one that follows perfectly from the discipline stage: Discourage and punish poor behavior; reward and encourage good behavior. It's a simple enough idea to follow, but one that can be difficult to execute properly. If you offer to let your child down for taking two more bites of food, as in the earlier example, then allowing them to get down without taking two more bites, regardless of the time that has passed or how much of a fit they're throwing, is quite possibly the worst thing you can do to that child.

Continuing with discipline at this stage can be difficult for many parents. Parents who spent what can seem like an eternity dedicating their efforts to firm discipline may be tempted to let up on the gas pedal a little bit and release some of that tight grip. Although each child and parent is different, and the ultimate goal for each child is to eventually remove all of the parental discipline, too much freedom in this stage can be detrimental to the process. We'll get to that freedom in the next stages of the model. The training stage is a consistent test of the discipline instilled in the child in the previous stage.

Understanding authority

We must teach our children to show respect for those in authority over us. Parents take center stage here, but we must be careful not to limit the scope of our child's influences. We must train the child that this respect for others goes far beyond parents and grandparents. We somehow must portray to our children that we, as parents, friends, adults, teachers, law enforcement officers, and all other authority figures, are part of a group of people that deserves equal respect. A key part of testing the discipline stage is ensuring that the child understands proper etiquette and how to behave in various situations in which they will encounter other sources of adult influence.

Consider the definition of training: Repeating a certain activity with the intent of achieving a specific result. Now consider your own life. Riding a bike may have come easy to you. There were probably a few bumps and bruises and a few skinned knees, but you picked up on it. You wouldn't have gotten through those first few hiccups without some persistence. No two people are the same, so some folks may have had a difficult time with this now seemingly simple task. We may have progressed from a tricycle, to a small bike with training wheels, to no training wheels, and eventually moving up to larger and larger bicycles. The time required to complete that process was short for some and longer for others. Much of the variables depend on the individual's drive and how much their parents pushed them. Regardless, the key for this process was persistence. Some people simply need more repetition than others.

Reid was a decent baseball player in his younger days. As a sophomore, he surpassed the batting average record on his high school varsity team, hitting an impressive .538. For those unfamiliar with baseball, that means he got on base more than half the time he stepped in the batter's box. The last person to hit over .400 in the major leagues was Ted Williams. It's said that Williams was so focused on hitting and practicing that he could tell the difference between the weight of his usual bat and one that was half an ounce heavier. He once sent some bats back to the manufacturer because they didn't feel right in his hands. Upon inspection, it was discovered that the handle area was five-one thousandths larger than it was supposed to be. How do you get to be that good at understanding hitting? The key is consistent practice and training. How did Reid accomplish such an impressive feat to reach that batting average? A great coach and a lot of practice.

Reid remembers most of his coaches quite well throughout his sports career. But none of them had the direct impact as noticeable as Matt Covey. Covey was an assistant coach during Reid's sophomore year and impacted his performance in a way that he'd never experienced. Covey broke down and analyzed hitting better than anyone Reid had known. Covey studied mechanics and techniques, the way the body aligned and moved, and where and how weight was positioned, and he had a system for how to do each correctly. Reid attributes his success that season to Covey's coaching. In his subsequent years, when Covey was not his coach, Reid's average slipped into the .400s—still impressive, but the decrease was surely due to the loss of his trainer.

Imitation plays a huge role in the training stage. When progressing through the logic model, the child goes from having no logic, to using his parents' logic, to using his own. At birth, we possess no logic of our own. While growing up, we must first use the logic and reasoning provided by our parents. As knowledge and logic are acquired, children still often lack the mental capacity to generate a complex thought process on their own. In the training stage, the parent relies heavily on their own logic and reasoning, laying the groundwork for the child to develop his or her own logic that will take over in later stages. It's this framework of logic that will be the basis for all of the child's own thought process as an adult. Because of this, imitation will play a large role in the training stage.

Teachable moments and modeling behavior

As parents we must be on high alert for both teachable moments and moments when we can model desired behavior to provide a good example for our children. Let's take a look at an example from the airport. Let's say you're on a trip and have just completed the first leg of your two-leg flight. You and the family are running around trying to keep your details, baggage, and kids in order while finding your new gate. You're on the move to your departing gate and little Mariah wants to help and be a big girl by pulling her own bag. If Mariah were not paying attention to her surroundings or how the bag is moving and were to trip another traveler, we've found a teachable moment. The right thing to do in this instance would be to stop Mariah and encourage (force if necessary) her to apologize to the nice elderly lady that she ran into. This is a great example of capitalizing on a teachable moment.

If, however, after forcing Mariah to apologize, you go off and start cursing (or worse) at the first person that cut in front of you in line at Burger King, you've instantly lost any benefit that came from Mariah's earlier teachable moment. You may have unintentionally caused confusion and distrust to spring up between you and Mariah. As parents, we need to be keenly aware of our own behavior, especially with children in the training stage. Imitation is a powerful tool, one that can help or hurt our efforts to get a child quickly through this stage in the model. It is both hypocritical and an unfair expectation to hold your child to a standard to which you are unwilling to hold yourself, even though, at times, it feels like the appropriate thing to do.

Parents must avoid rewarding bad behavior, and this may be one of the toughest parts of this process. Think back to the offer we extended at the dinner table a few moments ago. If little Suzy is unwilling to eat those two more bites or begins throwing a temper tantrum at the idea, the absolute worst thing we can do is change the offer. This is a game of chess, and your little one has the ability to be incredibly persistent. With the first inch you give, she's going to take a mile.

Think back to the previous chapter and the tantrum in the grocery store. The worst thing we can do in that situation would be to give in and buy that toy or candy bar in an effort to bring a quick end to the scene. Our first step, after telling our child "No" or asking them to do something (or stop doing something) is to calmly and collectively make an effort to explain why you're making that request. If that doesn't work, we're not only giving you permission to let your child throw that temper tantrum, we're encouraging you to do so. Let other folks judge if they want. The parents who understand the desire to properly train a child (or at least those who have read this book) will get it. And they may even provide a little word of encouragement. Now, there will be other parents that feel the opposite, too, and question your parenting style. These are the people who wonder and sometimes may even ask how you could be so mean. Don't waste time with the concerns of these people. They're the ones with kids that grow up to have no backbone, are spoiled, and cannot handle conflict as adults. You don't want those kids. You want good kids. Cry on, Suzy. Cry on.

Positive reinforcement

It's hard to do, but do not reinforce bad behavior. Do NOT give the kid the toy or the treat if they are misbehaving. At worst, be neutral towards bad behavior, but never reinforce it. Always condemn it and punish when you're able. Hear me on this. What we are not telling you to do is spank your child in the cereal aisle of the grocery store, not necessarily anyway. Think back to last chapter. With many folks being hyperaware and ultrasensitive these days, many people observing you may mistake your corporal punishment as if it were coming out of anger, not love, for that child. And some of those folks might call you out for it, or worse, call you in for child abuse. Don't worry, they had soft parents themselves and don't fully understand how this parenting thing works. That said, being a strong parent and punishing your children does not give you the right to disrespect your child. Many children, especially young children, are very soft and tenderhearted, even though they remind you more of an aisle 10 terrorist right now throwing that temper tantrum. Be respectful of their fragility. As discussed in the last chapter, there is a time and a place for punishment and discipline. That may very well be the cereal aisle of your local grocery store, but you might have a greater impact if you sat that child down out in the parking lot or at home and had a very adult-like conversation with them about why their behavior was unacceptable and the punishment they're going to receive as a result. Can you imagine how your child would react if every time they acted out and were disrespectful, your response was to treat them like an adult? It just might help them become one someday.

Similarly, during the training stage, it is absolutely vital that we as parents are prepared to follow through on any threat we make. Please read that sentence again. If you threaten something and the child does not respond, you have no other choice, zero options, but to do exactly as you said. If you threaten your child with a specific type of response or punishment for less than ideal behavior you must be fully prepared, 100-percent bought in, to follow up on that threat if your child's behavior doesn't improve. We need to carry out the result, both for ourselves and for the child. Ultimately, we need to deliver this in such a way that is not going to worsen the situation, at least not in the long term, and ensure that the desired behavior or outcome is achieved.

The training required for this portion may be more training for us as parents than for our kids. We may need to be extra cautious on the type of rewards or threats we're extending to our children. If you say, "I'm going to stop this car and let you out the next time you yell in the back seat," then you darn well better be prepared to follow through. The point we're trying to emphasize here is that it's worse for the child long-term to experience empty threats or promises than it is for short-term discomfort, like standing on the side of the road alone for two minutes. Another point for parents to consider in this stage is the frequency of threats like this. If you're dropping Timothy off on the side of the road every 45 minutes of a trip, there will be other adverse effects. He could be traumatized by the idea of repeatedly being left by his parents. The punishment or threat could also lose its impact after a few instances because he knows you'll eventually come back to pick him up. The only option when that happens is to escalate the punishment, and you'll quickly start down a slippery slope if you overuse any one tactic.

Here's another example: Tommy explains that he has a birthday party for a friend on Saturday, and we respond by telling him that he won't be able to go to the party with his friends unless his room is picked up by that morning. If Tommy's room is not picked up on Saturday morning, he does not get to go to the party. Plain and simple. End of story. Done deal. He doesn't get extra credit for something else. He doesn't get a second chance. No party.

Now, some of you may argue that the response is too aggressive or intense, but we promise that it is not—at least if you made the threat. In situations like these, we need to think back about our original goal. Ultimately, we want Tommy and all of our other kids to grow up to be active, engaged, competent, and contributing adults. What's worse in this situation? Tommy might miss one of his friends' 8th birthday party, or learn a valuable lesson about actions and consequences that will stick with him for the rest of his life. Let him miss the party. We promise, he'll get over it. He might even thank you for it one day. And he sure as heck will clean his room next time. That was the goal, was it not?

Stick with it

We must be fully willing to execute any form of punishment or threat we give our children. If we tell Suzy she must finish her beans before she goes to play after supper, and after five minutes of arguing we tell her that she only needs to eat three more bites, we've failed Suzy. Again, it may sound extreme or intense, but we can assure you that your child will progress through this stage and the next much more quickly if we are fully bought in to this idea. Also, how often have you fought that battle about the beans with Suzy? Too many, we'd suspect. Stick to your guns on this a few times and see how many more times Suzy decides to pick that battle. In the not-so-distant future, she'll learn that the bean battle is one from which she never seems to come out victorious and she will simply stop fighting it. On the flipside of that coin, we must be prepared to reward good behavior. This type of strong parenting may seem over-the-top for some of you (thank your own parents if that's the case), but it can and should be a very positive experience. Don't fight that bean battle more times than you have to. Don't fight it more than once if you can help it. Set Suzy on the straight-and-narrow path right away and move on. She'll be happier, and you'll certainly enjoy the family dinner table a lot more. Again, this process can and definitely should be a positive experience.

Lauren, Ron's daughter and Reid's wife, has a hilarious example of this process working out. The oldest of five kids, Lauren was

Ron and Renee's first attempt at parenting. There's a story that gets shared frequently around our dinner table about a time when Lauren was barely 2 years old. Ron had been giving her a bath, and after draining the water he told her she needed to pick up and put away her bath toys before she could get out of the tub. The defiant Lauren (some things never change) decided at that moment she was going to press the issue. She recalls vividly to this day her decision to "see what happens" when she doesn't listen to her father's requests. At 2 years old!

It was a winter night in an old country farmhouse and that little girl's face turned almost purple before she finally picked up that last little rubber ducky. She sat in that tub, stark naked, cold and wet, for almost two hours before she decided to comply. This was an enjoyable experience for no one in the house that night, but to this day, the experience gets brought up often about how much of a positive impact that had on her. Even as a toddler, she recalls learning a valuable lesson about listening to those in charge. And no, she wasn't scarred for life as some of you reading this are perhaps thinking. She willingly laughs about it and enjoys the conversation, often starting it herself, when recalling that story with others.

Outside influences

One thing we haven't discussed yet for the training stage is the importance of filtering outside influences from your child. There's a fine line here that parents must walk between sheltering their child and allowing them access to too many of the wrong outside influences. Your child will have friends, classmates, and neighbors that have parents who are likely not following this model, or anything even close. By no fault of your own, your child will encounter situations that disagree with this model and unintentionally counteract your efforts. It is crucial that we hold diligent about filtering those outside forces for your children, more so at this stage than any other. This can be the difference between starting the process over or graduating to the next phase, in which the child takes on more responsibility.

One nice thing about this stage is that the majority of time spent with these friends, classmates, and neighbors is done under parental supervision. Because of the age of these children (at least if you started this process at birth), your sons and daughters will need both permission and assistance with making arrangements to get together with their friends. As parents going through this model, we can take advantage of this situation and hold a level of control in their friendships. We have the ability to interview and observe who they're interacting and beginning friendships with. Although you may not always feel like it, offer to host a get-together for your child and his or her friends. These situations often offer up a great deal of teachable moments, as we can help them understand how to choose their friends and teach them about which traits are important in friendships and other relationships.

Failing to take advantage of the teaching moments like the grocery store temper tantrums unintentionally push us back a step. If this takes place too often while in the training stage, we must hit the pause and rewind buttons. During the training stage, you will have moments in which Suzy presses the issue and is lying on the floor in the grocery store or at the dinner table kicking and screaming. If you give in, you're automatically required to go back to the discipline stage and relearn a few lessons for Suzy. If you succeed, the teachable moment can be crucial to the training stage.

Let's return again to the metaphor of riding a bike. The training stage would be comparable to riding a bike with training wheels.

By this point, you've got the basic understanding and strategy down: pedal and you move forward, turn the wheel left and you go this direction, stop pedaling and you stop moving forward, turn the wheel right and you go that direction. Pretty simple, right? But once that understanding is present, that child can graduate to a more "adult-like" bicycle with the assistance of training wheels. Training wheels take that basic understanding a level further and begin to teach position and balance. It also usually means the child is able to cover more ground in a shorter amount of time. Even when this starts to happen, keep in mind that this process is a marathon, not a sprint. Lance Armstrong had training wheels at one point, too. It's not until there is complete understanding and a confidence of that understanding that we begin to remove those training wheels.

When you feel you're ready to transition from the training to coaching stages, let your children know. Don't hesitate to be candid with them and tell them that because of their great behavior, respect, and performance lately, you're going to begin giving them a bit more freedom. This will be welcomed with open arms for many of your children, not to mention begin (if you haven't already) a relationship that's built on trust and transparency with your child.

For a few out there, though we'd suspect a much smaller group, this new freedom will be met with a bit of hesitation or resistance. If that's the case, and you truly feel your child isn't ready for that next step in the progression of this model, don't let them off the hook quite yet. If the concerns are legitimate, spend a bit more time ensuring that the concepts in this chapter have sunk in with your child. At the same time, we'd encourage you to make sure you're not holding them back from taking those next steps toward growth. Allowing your children to progress to the next phase of this relationship model is a fantastic gift. You'd be doing them a disservice by not allowing them to do that based on your own fear. Let them know that they're not alone. As you prepare to move from training to coaching, do some scrimmages. Run through a few scenarios. "Here's what's going to happen, here's what I'm expecting, but you're not alone. I'm right here if you need me." Coaching takes that next level of communication and transparency and says, "I can't shoot the free throw for you or come out onto the court and move that guy out of your way, but I can encourage you from the sideline, remind you of the proper form, and help you use what you've learned to solve the problem for yourself. It's time to sink or swim on your own."

— CHAPTER THREE —

Coaching

After passing through the discipline stage and graduating from the training stage, you and your child will enter the coaching phase. This is an exciting part of the journey as our children can take significant strides in maturity during this portion of the process. That said, coaching (like every stage in the model) carries unique challenges for both parent and child. Each stage also requires parents to relinquish a bit more control to allow our children to take on new responsibilities. As described in the past chapters, each growth moment provides new forms of freedom. The coaching stage is the first taste of real freedom for many children. And this freedom prompts some parents to struggle the most with this stage.

A great example of setting the stage for this part of our process is Reid's mom, Sheri, and what she does in her classroom each year. She has been a 3rd- and 4th-grade teacher for as many years as Reid can remember. At the onset of each school year she takes a few moments to set the tone for the year. She explains to her students, mostly 8- to 10-year-olds, that they now have larger responsibilities. They aren't in 1st or 2nd grade anymore. They are growing and maturing, and as a result will have both new freedoms and higher expectations. As mentioned at the close of the previous chapter, you can do this with your own children. And you can do it much earlier than age 8.

Before we go any further explaining the coaching phase and all of its wonderful characteristics, allow us to point out one very specific and important detail. Just because this stage is called the coaching phase does not mean that a new coach or teacher enters the equation and you as parents are any more off the hook or any less involved. The important thing to realize here is that you as a parent are equally responsible for your role in this stage as you have been in the previous two stages, and just as you will be in the remaining two stages. Rather, we as parents must be willing to adjust and modify our previous roles with each new stage in the process.

One of Reid's favorite things growing up was being a member of a sports team. Whether it was baseball, basketball, football, soccer, or anything else, he absolutely loved being involved with a team. He loved being able to walk out of a locker room wearing the same jersey, the same colors, the same uniform as 15 other guys knowing full well that they were working together to pursue a common goal. The guy standing next to him knew that equally well, and they all played a unique role in the equation. The guy sitting next to him, the same. Having a role on a team, playing a unique position, and providing a unique value to the group is one of the most amazing things to be a part of, especially as a young child. We could go into all of the wonderful benefits and life lessons children learn being involved in these types of activities at a young age, but that could fill another text completely.

The player-coach

Few people talk about how the family environment can function just like that team. The family group is comprised of various players and various positions, each with a unique contribution, each with a unique perspective and experience. As a parent in this situation, you fill the role of a player-coach. Early on, during this stage, your focus will be more on being a coach or instructor, but as we progress into later stages of the model your role will continue to shift as you become less of a coach and more of a teammate for your child. For now, your goal as a coach is to take that group of individuals in your family (your spouse, kids, etc.) and move toward a team environment in your home.

When we remember that we're all playing for the same team, it enables team members to overcome tiny obstacles or errors and continue progressing toward our goals. As parents, this allows us to approach situations our families face with a teaching mindset. This mindset will prepare us to take advantage of the coachable moments in our everyday lives. It will allow us to capitalize in the best way possible on small opportunities to have a big impact on our children and their future.

Great coaches create the environment that we described a few paragraphs earlier. This environment quickly provides a sense of belonging for each team member. Your family team is no different. As parents, our role is to create structure and foundation, provide boundaries as well as encouragement, support, and grace. All of these things allow for a child to gain a wonderful sense of belonging within the team and the family environment. Imagine the difference in our families, schools, and communities if every child had that sense of belonging to the various teams and groups in which they find themselves. There is no greater place for this to start than in our homes. The best model exists within our very own families.

Recognize here that just because we're now all on a team, we won't suddenly all get along. We all bring different viewpoints, attitudes, and perspectives, and there's a good chance of disagreement among team members. This is true even though we may all agree on striving for the same goal. There will be differences of opinions as to how to best to achieve that goal, and good coaches understand the need for balance. They do this by adding some new-found flexibility to the rigid structure they've created. Good coaches understand the need for a linear progression through the learning model, combined with personalization for the development of each unique team member.

Scrimmages

The next phase of this model is often the point that is most difficult for parents. It's at this stage, the coaching stage, where free will begins to set in on the part of the child. Until this point, we've been forcing our children to use our logic because of their inability to logically process most things on their own. Coaching marks the beginning of a shift in the ownership of that logic.

To many, coaching is the launching phase for their children. It's the trial run, the dress rehearsal. This attitude and approach provide a confirmation that the earlier steps are complete and our children are ready to begin the journey into adulthood, into maturity. This is the stage in which logic begins to become our children's own.

Think of this stage through the example of a basketball team. A coach is very hands-on in practice, out there on the court with the team providing specific instruction as to what to do and what behavior is expected while running a great deal of situational exercises to ensure players understand the concepts. It's at this stage that we can be hands-on as coaches, showing and demonstrating how to handle situations. But as we progress through the coaching stage of the model, we enter the moment when we begin to put our children through real-life scenarios on their own. We begin to run scrimmages.

During these scrimmages, we provide practice opportunities to simulate real life or game scenarios. We do this because the game is ultimately what we're preparing for. In order to apply the concepts we've learned through our practices and drills, we have to run trials, or scrimmages, as a way to offer real-time feedback and verify whether or not the lessons we're teaching have sunk in to the point in which our children can practically apply them. Ultimately, this leads to a game scenario in which coaches are left on the sidelines and it's up to the team and the individuals to perform, apply lessons learned, and execute the strategy and tactics that have been worked on during regular practice sessions.

We can also compare this to preparing for a concert or a theater play. Coaches in this instance instruct participants during practices with specific feedback and critiques on how to improve their performance. We repeat these steps, lessons, and individual and group practice sessions until we get the desired behavior to take place naturally and they begin to become habit. And all of these practices and dress rehearsals prepare us for the big show.

A perfect example of this for our family was when Kylen, the youngest of Ron and Renee's kids, was being courted by a nice young man and she was seeking dating advice. Kylen was relatively new to the scene (as parents, Ron and Renee withheld that from their children until they were at least 16) and was eager for some input from her family. The young man who was pursuing her was doing all the right things and making all the right moves. And likely not the moves you're thinking. He and Kylen had a number of conversations about the possibility of dating. At one point he had called Ron to ask permission to date his daughter, and he even came to the house to visit with Ron and Renee together about it. All the while, Kylen was on the fence.

It's nice to be desired. We want to be wanted. And this guy had a lot of things going for him. Yet there were a few things working against him. With the solid foundation laid by Ron and Renee, Kylen was well-aware of what a strong, cohesive marriage looked like. And by watching her older sisters over the years, she was at least somewhat aware of the impacts of making questionable choices when it comes to dating. That in mind, Kylen was tuned in to the fact that there were enough yellow flags to cause potential concern. His home life and upbringing were quite different than what she was familiar with. His religious views were also different, something that's very important to Kylen and the whole family. Different enough that Kylen admitted to knowing she'd never end up marrying him.

When it came time to offer counsel on this particular situation, Ron and Renee had similar thoughts, that it probably wasn't in Kylen's best interest. But because of her age and the stage in their relationship, Ron and Renee offered their input and left it at that. Kylen recalls a pivotal moment in a conversation with her dad up in her room where he told her that they would support her either way, whatever the decision. He also made a point to remind her that the following year, when she'd head off to college, she'd be making a lot more choices like this on her own. And she'd continue to do so for the rest of her life. Ultimately, Kylen chose not to pursue the relationship. When it comes to dating, you'll either end up breaking up or getting married. Kylen couldn't see herself doing the latter, and so chose to save herself from doing the former and avoided taking the relationship further.

This is where we find ourselves in the model as coaches. We've had ample opportunity to show, instruct, and direct our children; however, we are also now beginning to limit ourselves to only participate from the sidelines in various scenarios. We can no longer be on the court or the field full-time and correct the misbehavior of our children in the moment. We have reached a pivotal point in the model where the actions and behavior of our children have become their own. Likewise, the consequences are equally theirs. The child is in the arena, on the field, actively making decisions on his or her own. We've entered a fantastic phase during which behavior is based on the child's own reasoning, judgment, and ideas, not someone else's. No matter how badly we want to be in control, this launching phase is of critical importance to the mature development of our children. We absolutely must give up control, or we will suddenly become our own worst enemy. If we are unwilling to give up control in this phase, we are slowing the growth and development of our children—or worse, preventing it completely.

It's during this stage that our participation can only come from the sidelines as instruction. We're no longer able to demonstrate or manipulate out on the field of play. This highlights the significance of ensuring that the discipline and training phases are complete and we've provided ample time and practice in the coaching phase before launching into any later stages. Here in the coaching phase, we're again going to stretch the boundaries we've set up for our kids. In this phase we will provide direction from a distance. We need to remember, though, that aspects from all of the other stages still apply. Kids should be coachable after being properly disciplined and trained in the earlier portions of the model. We will begin to allow for our children to apply their own logic at this stage. That means we're saying things like, "We're not going to stop you from doing Activity XYZ, but as your coach I'm going to discourage you," based on some specific reasoning. As hard as it may be, we need to move to this stage and leave that discipline stage or we'll stifle the free spirit and freethinking of our children.

How we got here and where we're going

Let's consider our model so far as we continue to compare it to a team sport activity. Discipline can be thought of as getting into athletic shape. It is the beginning of the entire process that sets the foundation—doing the necessary, but difficult, job of getting into appropriate shape. Training is the progression into practicing what we've learned, and coaching transitions to scrimmages, real-life simulations, and trial-running our children's own logic. The mentorship phase begins after all the skills and fundamentals are understood and rehearsed, and our children repeatedly apply the lessons learned in the previous three stages.

Now, let's not forget about the ability to call a time out or return to hold another practice session. As a coach, although we are not able to control the game ourselves out on the field of play, we can call for a temporary break to remind our children of the lessons they've been taught. We have these trial runs and time outs for a reason. Coaching is the final stage when we as parents remain present as a safety net and an instructor. It's the beginning of the transition to adulthood, but not the end of the process. Coaching is the final stage in which the parent has any enforceable role. We still are able to adjust and correct misbehavior. Any behaviors that require more than a small adjustment mean we may have to temporarily revisit the training stage. Later, we will remove this safety net completely as we progress to the mentoring phase. The mentoring stage removes the ability to provide any recourse or punishment, but we're not quite there yet.

It's at this point we'd like to make one important note. You've maybe heard it said that, "Uncoachable kids make unemployable adults." We couldn't agree more. As much fun as it would be to turn our kids loose and have them be on their own, spending enough time in the coaching stage, like each of the five phases, is of vital importance. Coaches of top athletes agree that the greatest talent on the team, if unwilling to work or unwilling to listen and learn, will make things incredibly difficult. We've all seen these types of people and maybe even worked with them—the know-it-all. We must instill in our children an attitude of lifelong learning that will prevent them from ever being "that guy" as an adult. In this portion of our process, we still have the ability to critique, offer feedback, and provide suggestions. And it's the final part of our model in which we can do this from a foundation of authority. The subsequent stages transition full and complete ownership of that authority to our children. Because of that, it's critical we run ample scrimmages and trials with our children during coaching.

Reid's dad, also named Ron, coached many of Reid's recreation-league teams growing up. Reid's parents made a point to be actively involved in the lives of Reid and his sister. This often meant that Reid's dad was in the dugout or the sidelines. Whether he was a formal coach of Reid's team or not, it never failed that he'd help Reid analyze the situation after games or practices were over. Ron would also ask great leading questions. He'd force Reid to reflect and consider what could've been improved or what he might do next time in a given situation. This is what great coaches do. Ron was a true coach, on and off the field. An excellent athlete and competitor himself, he often had the answers, but he'd help Reid get there on his own because that's what great coaches do. They teach you how to learn and grow. They teach you how to begin an inward development and improvement process, and they use specific tasks or activities like music, chores, or sports to establish that system.

Practical application

So what does the practical application of the coaching phase look like? As we mentioned, it begins the transition of logic and reason over to the child. For example, it's during this stage that we could consider allowing our children to determine their own curfews. There's a trust factor that enters in the coaching phase, and in this example, the curfew now becomes up to them. As parents, that means when asked by our child, "When do you want me home?" we now have the ability to say things like, "I want you home at an appropriate time." This is a transfer of ownership of the decision and an offer of trust to the child. This is a signal to the child that we believe we've provided enough foundation and instruction in the past that they can now use their own logic and reasoning to determine an acceptable curfew. For their sake and our own, we must rely on the lessons of the past and their knowledge and understanding of what we've taught them thus far to determine the best action and understand possible recourse.

Consider again our example from an earlier chapter—the melt down in the grocery store. Parents frequently fall victim to themselves in these situations. They succumb to emotion and focus their concern on their own self-preservation rather than the lessons we wish to send to our child. We begin thinking thoughts like, "People are judging me. People think I'm a terrible parent." This couldn't be further from the truth. We must remember, especially in the coaching stage, that it's about the child, not us. We'll get out to the car and any embarrassment we felt will quickly fade as we merge into traffic and deal with everything else ahead. We must not be afraid to take advantage of the coachable moments, even if they are incredibly public.

Continuing with the curfew example, it's important to note that if we extend the invitation for our child to determine their own curfew, we must allow them the freedom to act accordingly. And yes, that does mean that if they say 2 a.m. seems appropriate, we allow them to actually make that decision for themselves. That's not to say we cannot still coach them by providing guidance or input, but we must reassure the child that we are not going to make that decision for them. As long as it's within reason, we should comply with their desired curfew. If it's out of line or you truly feel their request is out of bounds, have an adult-like conversation to come to some sort of compromise.

Unless they begin to abuse the freedom and consistently make poor decisions, this should be our regular and consistent approach to their questions. Sending these "I trust you even though I may not completely agree with you" signals often and repeatedly is a steady form of encouragement for proper behavior for our kids. In the event things don't go perfectly the first few times, we still need to ensure that we don't immediately react by re-engaging the training stage. The coaching stage still allows for adjustments to be made, but they are smaller in size. At the coaching level, discipline and recourse should also be transferred over to our child. Often the larger lesson is learned in self-correcting poor behavior than the mistake itself. Back to our example: "You stayed out until 3 a.m. last night, that's against the rules. What do you think is the appropriate consequence?" At the coaching level we must also begin to transform parental discipline into self-discipline.

Punishment vs. recourse

It's important to note here that the coaching level also carries another interesting transition. At this point, we must make the distinction between punishment and recourse. This is the stage in which punishment and consequences begin to coexist but are now two separate and distinct items. This may get muddy, so bear with us. Consequences, or recourse, and punishment can be the same, or result in the same type of reprimand, but they can also prompt two separate reactions. For example, as parents we want to transition over to conversations with our kids about consequences in the coaching phase. In previous stages, our conversations revolved more around punishment for poor behavior. To help clarify the difference we need to remove the negative feelings we have toward the word consequences. We need to remember that consequences can be positive as well as negative. The consequence for studying is likely a higher grade on a test. Likewise, the consequence for not studying is most likely a lower grade on a test.

That distinction continues as we work with our children to improve misbehavior during this stage of the model. It looks like this: "We're not necessarily going to discipline you for your behavior (punishment), but you've gotten yourself into a predicament here and there will be consequences for whatever you choose." Punishing at this stage is less about teaching and discipline and more about reinforcement of the system. At this stage, any punishment is likely short term and consequences are longer term.

Consider if your child gets in trouble for being a minor in possession of alcohol. There is a difference between potential punishment and potential consequences. Punishment could be the loss of a vehicle or grounding for a month. Consequences on the other hand likely have a larger impact. This could be the loss of a scholarship or high car-insurance rates. It could also look like failing to get into the university the child wanted because they were unwilling to put in the time studying.

We must also not forget to highlight what a positive example of this looks like. For that we look to Olivia, Ron and Renee's second oldest. Likely the most obedient of the Olson children, Olivia was a hard worker that had little trouble setting her sights on future goals at the cost of immediate rewards. Ron and Renee had slightly different opinions on whether or not they should pay for their kids' college education. They compromised and committed to covering a portion of the costs for each child. As part of the arrangement with their kids, they also shared that if any of the kids were to receive a full-ride scholarship to college, they would still honor their commitment to provide financial assistance in other areas. Buying them a new car, for example, as a reward for their hard work. This offer, and the associated challenge, worked particularly well as motivation for Olivia who would go on to receive a full ride scholarship.

Where the story takes an interesting twist, though, is what Olivia chose to do with that reward she was promised. Rather than go out and buy a brand-new car as an 18-year-old, which would've been awfully exciting, Olivia chose to settle for a used car at a significantly lower price. Through some coaching and conversations with her parents, the three of them agreed to use a portion of the available funds to cover the cost of a lesser expensive vehicle and reserve the additional sum to someday assist with the down payment on a home. The decision was hers. And if you'd ask her today, she'd tell you it was one of many her parents helped coach her through, even as a teenager, that has had a lasting positive impact on her life.

Coaching can be an incredibly enjoyable experience as a parent. This doesn't mean that the other stages are not enjoyable, but as you watch the child mature and witness their own logic and decision-making process begin to take shape, it is an unbelievably rewarding experience. This is as true in the coaching phase of our model as it is in any other phase. Parents can typically take partial credit for the great things going on in their children's lives, but coaching is the final stage of active participation. As we progress to the mentorship and friendship stages, the amount of participation we have significantly changes. Rather, we begin to share in the joy of our children's lives from a mutual standpoint rather than as through an instructor-student type relationship.

— CHAPTER FOUR —

Mentorship

Welcome to the mentorship phase. As parents progressing through the model in our relationships with our kids, many consider this to be the most enjoyable stage of all. It's here in the mentorship stage that we as parents move into an ally role. We now operate more in a supportive role as opposed to being an active participant in the daily ins-and-outs of our children's lives. Until this stage, we've held an enforceable role with our children, at least on some level. That authority is stripped away in the mentorship phase, and if done well it can be equally enjoyable for the parent and the child.

It's no secret that some parents will be better at this stage than others. As in every other stage, certain parents will find success substantially more quickly than others. Please note here that this is an issue on the part of the parent, not the child.

In our model, the mentorship phase is fundamentally the release of our children. As parents, it is here that we will begin to release control of our children. This is the last stage at which you have a separation from your child in terms of the roles you play, those being of the superior and the subordinate, but that difference is so little. Adulthood will not be successful if we only offer our children a limited release in the mentorship phase. We may want to let them go off and enjoy the world as adults, but if Suzy still considers Mom and Dad as her emergency fund and backup plan, that release has not been a successful one.

Here in stage four of our model, we have the final opportunity to take our children into full adulthood. Everything we've done up to this point will begin to culminate in the mentorship phase as our child takes more ownership and responsibility for themselves than they ever have before. It's in this stage that we have our final opportunity to have an impact on our children through a separation of roles, albeit in the form of much smaller changes than in the earlier stages. At this stage, we can only mold and tweak—not modify and manipulate. Think of a sculptor crafting a vase or bowl out of clay. Nearing the final stages, we can only take off a rough edge or sand down a minor blemish. We've passed the point in which we can change the overall shape. That is fully established at this point, and we're left to make small tweaks and final adjustments.

The roles of influencer and decision-maker switch during this stage. The decision-making role flip-flops here, and now the decision-making power rests completely with the child, not the parent. As parents, we now fill the role of providing input, much like the child did in the earlier stages. We can provide our thoughts, give advice and examples of what we would do or would have done in similar situations, but the decision ultimately rests with the child. In coaching and earlier stages, the parents own the decision and the child has an influence. In mentorship, the child holds the decision-making power and the parent has the ability to provide influence, but little more. This is the graduation—not necessarily a single event, but it happens somewhere in the child's maturation process. This letting go of the decision-making power is a paradigm shift in the parent-child relationship. This shifting, this transition, is something that will come much easier for some parents, while many others will find this to be the most difficult step in our entire process.

Many of you reading this will find this to be a simple process. You've been working hard for some time now and ultimately knew that this was the goal you were working toward. For those of us that fall into this category, we need to remember that, even in the mentorship phase, we still need to follow a few rules and we still play a critical role.

On the other side of the spectrum, many of you reading this will find the mentorship phase to be the most difficult to execute. Moms more typically than dads may struggle while entering the mentorship phase, because it can be seen as the end of the road as the child's parent in the traditional sense, the giving up of our unique role as caretaker and caregiver. We urge you to feel just the opposite. An eagle that is never allowed to jump out of the tree will never know if he or she can truly fly on their own. Plus, the nest would get crazy crowded, and that's a lot of mouths to keep feeding every day. But unlike with an eagle, this releasing of our children will not come in a single event. It should be a very natural easy process over time.

Fairness

Ultimate success as a parent will be noticed in fits and flashes throughout this stage as your child progresses to fully thinking and operating on their own. The mistake that many parents make in the mentorship stage is they feel it's the last opportunity to make Me Version 2.0. Hear this: The goal is not to replicate yourself in your children. They are their own individual persons with unique strengths, assets, ideas, and skills. Remember that each player on a team fills a unique role and offers unique perspective and value. This is the stage at which we need to help them reach their full potential, not yours. We need to help them become the best version of themselves, not the best miniature version of yourself.

It is at the mentorship phase that we will cater to the bent of the child more than any other. We need to begin allowing for some ideas, logic, and desires of our children more than our own, even if we disagree with them. That's how development works.

This concept may be best explained in terms of fairness, and what is considered fair. Reid's sister, Amber, is a great golfer—good enough to beat anyone in the family on a given day. In high school when Amber was on the golf team and volleyball team, Reid was playing basketball, football, soccer, baseball, track, and golf. It was a wild and chaotic time for Reid and for his parents. Reid remembers vividly one day when his sister, and their mother were shopping for basketball shoes in the local sporting goods store in Sioux Falls, Scheels. His parents' policy up to this point was, in an effort to keep things fair for us (and likely in an effort to keep within the family budget), that we were allowed to get one new pair of sports shoes per year. These shoes then became our regular street shoes after we were done with them. Reid and his sister had a breakthrough moment on that shopping trip. While she may not remember the day at all, Reid sees it very clearly. He knows where they were standing, what part of the store, and the specific pair of Allen Iverson basketball shoes he was holding and asking his mom to help purchase.

While trying to convince his mother to spend the unnecessary amount of money on that pair of shoes, Reid's sister pointed out to their mother in a very straight-forward and matter-of-fact way that it would not be "fair" to hold Reid to a standard of one new pair of sport shoes per year if that's what she was allowed. He was participating in six sports. (To this day, Reid doesn't know how his family was able to make that work.) She played two. Fairness in this instance meant equality, not similarity. There is a very profound and simple distinction to be made there. Someone with even a basic understanding of mathematics could make the argument that Amber was getting a much better offer.

Now, we would also be the first to argue that if a child wants something so desperately and a parent says no, the child should have every right to get a job and earn the money to pay for those shoes or whatever item they have their hearts set on. It's a fine balance to walk and one that must be walked carefully and intentionally.

A map vs. a chauffer

Let's consider the modern GPS, or Global Positioning System. A GPS in our vehicle or phone will tell you where to go. It will give you specific instructions on how to arrive at your destination, but it's not going to actually get you there. In the mentorship phase, parents must act like that GPS. We're sitting in the passenger seat of the car providing some direction at appropriate times. We are, however, no longer driving the vehicle. That spot is being filled by the child we've been training and equipping all along. Parents no longer have control of the steering wheel or the throttle. Again, we are able to provide direction and input, but ultimately the control is in the child's hands. That doesn't mean we aren't involved. We may need to step in and help them recalculate the route at times based on some poor decisions, but we never take over driving.

An interesting example of this came when Lauren was in college. At that time sophomores at the University of Sioux Falls weren't allowed to live off-campus unless they lived at home. Conveniently enough, the IRS was allowing for a first-time homebuyers tax credit of $8,000. Those two facts, and a number of others, led Lauren to purchase a house. With Ron and Renee's help and support, Lauren was able to take advantage of the large tax credit, start building equity in a property of her own, and learn the process and responsibility that comes along with owning a home at an age younger than many who take that step. Oh, and she was also able to live off-campus. (This is a big deal at 19 years old.)

Lauren was a homeowner at 19 years old, working part-time hours around a full-time college schedule. That wouldn't be possible without a great mentoring effort. Ron and Renee helped work through the purchase details, ensured everything was being set up correctly, and turned Lauren loose. Very shortly, she had the house filled with roommates who were paying rent. She was making mortgage payments, scheduling maintenance, and doing everything else that goes along with homeownership. That doesn't happen by accident.

To this day, we believe that this was one of the better decisions Lauren and her parents made for her. Allowing roommates to help cover her mortgage payment with their rent each month was a great system. The lessons learned throughout those early years were invaluable. And they wouldn't have been possible without the mentorship model that Ron and Renee followed.

This type of mentorship requires something we'll call being actively disengaged, or participatively withdrawn. This is when mentors offer help and guidance when and where it's needed or solicited by the mentee, then back off and let the circumstances play out.

Hug the monster

In the mentorship phase, it's time to hug the monster. When you're in there up-close, it's warm and soft and fuzzy but still a monster. It stinks sometimes, might be a little dirty, but it's kind of comfortable, too. In this stage you'll say things to your child like, "You need a checking account. You need a car. I'm not going to do those things for you, but will mentor you through the process." There is a transition that takes place in your child during this phase. Together with your child, you are creating an adult version of their old self. Help them take on more responsible, adult-like things. As a sophomore in college, Ron and Renee mentored Lauren through the process of buying her first house. She filled it with roommates and managed all of the details herself, under their guidance. Because of the work-hard-and-be-rewarded attitude they instilled in their kids, Olivia was able to get a full-ride scholarship to school. And following through on their commitment, Ron and Renee agreed to purchase a new car for her in exchange for her achieving that goal. To take that example even further, because of the training mentioned earlier, rather than blow all of the money her parents had set aside for her schooling on a new car, Olivia chose to buy a nice, used vehicle and set aside the remainder as a way to help her and Josh make a larger down payment on their first house. These things don't happen simply by luck and good fortune. They require planning, training, diligence, and let's not forget some providence for these things to be accomplished.

— CHAPTER FIVE —

Friendship

Of all the steps in this model, the friendship stage is the easiest—at least it should be by this point. And if you've found yourself in a relationship with a child or parent having gone through all of the other stages, then congratulations are in order. You've made it to the destination. Getting to this stage should be the goal of every parent-child relationship. If you've made it to this point, you've hit the target you have been shooting for throughout the entire life of your child. When they were a toddler, our goal as parents was to produce a healthy, contributing adult. This is likely completed if you've reached this stage in our model. The skills, knowledge, and relationship are there. Ideally, this is a joyous, fun relationship for the rest of your life. Although it is true that this stage contains the least amount of difficulty, we're not done quite yet. There are still a few key things we need to check off the list.

It is said that friends are the family you choose. We believe choosing friends as adults is one of the most important things parents do. Your friends will be the other adults your kids look up to, those other examples besides Mom and Dad with new and unique perspectives, ideas, thoughts, and behavior. As parents, we need to ensure that we are picking and choosing the right people to include in that elite group of people we're willing to help nurture our kids. We need to surround ourselves, and our children, with the best possible support system we can create.

As a parent, there is a key behavior that needs to take place in this final stage. It's the parent's obligation to let the transition equality take place in its entirety—full release, complete equality. If you question such things as the purchase of a boat, the vacation to France, or the career choices of your child, you're not allowing for the complete release of the position of authority you once held over your child. You're withholding the full release. You're still trying to maintain an unnatural hold on things of the past, not allowing the full maturation of your child in the process.

The defining realization that you have entered this stage with a child is that the parent and child are now equals. At the friendship stage, neither parent nor child has a superior role in the relationship. While many of you would argue that little Timmy will always be your baby or that Suzy will never stop being your little girl, when you've arrived at this stage, they have done exactly that. No one will argue the unique relationship that parents have with their children. The relationship a mother has with her son or a father has with his daughter is always a special and indescribable thing. But friendship is a mutually held status. It's a place where both parties hold equal position and can contribute to the lives of each other at a similar level.

It is at this stage, if not sooner, that parents no longer question (unless providing advice or feedback about a particular situation) the decisions of their children. The relationship is 100-percent mutual. The hierarchy and superiority are gone. Going forward, the entire relationship and the rest of the results from the relationship come as a collection of the two parts blending, not the one having more influence or authority over the other.

By now, this child is no longer a child. He or she has their own unique experiences to draw from, their own perspective and outlook, and perhaps most importantly, their own unique set of skills, abilities, and insight they can bring to the relationship.

Unique experiences and perspectives

One story that always makes me laugh about Lauren is the time she and her sister, Olivia, spent in Europe while in college. Olivia and Lauren are two years apart and attended the same university. This allowed them to take a trip to Europe together over J-Term. For those unfamiliar with the model, J-Term is a three-week period in January that takes place between the two formal semesters of the school year, allowing students to take a condensed version of a course they need to complete or do a short focus on an area of interest. For many, this often means travel. On this trip, Lauren and Olivia found themselves in the middle of a busy square in Paris. They had been warned by a tour guide to watch their belongings and be mindful of potential pickpockets. When Olivia felt a quick tug at her purse, she announced to the group that someone was attempting to steal her valuables. Lauren, who is the oldest but shortest of the Olson clan, realized that her bag had already been gone through. Her wallet, ID, travel information, camera, and a number of other valuables were missing. Glancing up, the culprits were quickly walking away. The spitfire that she is, Lauren was not about to have any of that. She chased down the group of assailants while the others shouted, "Police." Getting in the face of these unknown assailants might not have been advisable, but that's exactly what she did. They denied involvement for a time, but eventually emptied their own pockets and threw all of Lauren's valuables on the ground.

What does this story have to do with parenting? Well other than getting that firecracker spirit from her mother, Renee, not a whole lot. However, that experience, like many others, has taught Lauren a few valuable lessons. In doing so, Lauren has also been able to reflect and share the experience with all of us around her. That's a situation we hope none of you ever find yourselves in. And we're not recommending chasing strangers down dark alleys in unfamiliar areas (definitely not encouraging that) but Lauren chose not to be a victim that day. And although her siblings, friends, and parents may never face those particular circumstances, you can rest assured anyone who hears that story coming from a tiny, fair-skinned blonde might gain a bit of confidence for himself.

That experience provides Lauren with a unique perspective that few will ever have. Her parents understand that. And they value the opinion and perspective that experiences like this have given her. There are likely hundreds of stories like that in her life and in your life that shape each and every one of us. All of us have a set of experiences that influence how we operate in the world. This is true for all of us, all of our family members, all of our friends, and everyone we interact with anywhere in the world. Those experiences are invaluable. Big or small, our unique circumstances and experiences shape who we become, and, as a result, each of us can provide valuable insight, feedback, and opinions to those around us.

When it comes to topics on confidence or boldness, you can bet our family knows who to talk to if we're seeking a bit of motivation—the fire-cracker, shorty, oldest child that wanted her wallet back.

We're all students. We're all teachers.

As mentioned, friendship is not JUST where you arrive and it's not a place where we can stop making an effort. The critical component for this stage is that it allows for the revelation and reflection of how to improve and repeat the process. It is collectively revisiting the entire process and relationship thus far. It's more than simply sharing the good times and great experiences. It is those things, but it's also about being able to discuss how to better improve this process overall, to examine the model that the two of you have gone through together, and potentially make modifications.

One very cool fact about this stage is that there is no longer a student-teacher relationship. Both parties involved now play both roles. This is the player part of the player-coach role we described in the coaching phase. The parent and the child are now both students, and they are now both teachers. As parents, your kids will have skills and talents that you do not. Think about that for a second. This person, now likely an adult, that you raised, that you helped teach, shape, and mold into the person they are today, has likely surpassed you in certain, if not most, areas. This is something to celebrate! Even though they are essentially a product of your doing, they've gone beyond what you were capable of teaching or sharing with them and now have a library of their own unique talents, ideas, skills, knowledge, and abilities. How cool is that?! Isn't that what we want for all of our kids? The best part about the friendship stage of the model is that both parties get to take advantage of those multiple skillsets and perspectives. What this allows us to do is combine them for the good of the whole.

The friendship stage is rooted in a mutual relationship, so both parties are capable of sharing the failures of the other without condemning. It's here that we can be more analytical than apologetic. A parent no longer needs to apologize in order to show a child how to own up to mistakes and be a better person. Instead, we're able to have a genuine conversation around some of the missteps we've taken as parents and in which areas of the model we might encourage modification. This is only doable here because both parties likely see the full picture. It's here that we tell our children to learn from our mistakes rather than making the same mistakes themselves. They will have a natural bent to make the same mistakes you did (because you were their instructor.) Now they have the opportunity to provide their own children with more tools.

The student becomes the teacher. This is the stage in the model in which, if we looked at the bottle, the directions would say, "Lather. Rinse. Repeat." Our children now have the opportunity to adjust the techniques inside this model and apply it to their own children. With our help and their perspectives on what worked well or didn't work well, we can make necessary tweaks to the system and continue improving the system. Life is a cumulative process. As the saying goes, history repeats itself. Without this reflection step, our children are destined to continue repeating the same mistakes we have made. Taking time to reflect and refresh the model is the critical step we can take to guarantee our children and their children are repeating only the best parts of their upbringing, not the worst.

Although this may seem like a simple notion for some, for others it may be incredibly profound. Let's consider the snowball effect. Good parenting, like bad parenting, has an exponential effect on future generations. Imagine the child that grew up in a broken home or a difficult parental situation. For some readers, this might not be difficult to imagine at all because it accurately describes our childhood. For others, we think of that one family or that one friend growing up that never quite had an ideal home life or relationship with their parents. Statistics show that unless corrective action is taken, we will repeat the same process as our parents as we raise our own children. Good, bad, or otherwise, we will most likely take a similar path as our parents when dealing with our own kids. It's time to buck that trend, especially if there are components of our childhood we'd rather forget than repeat. Let's instead create a system where perpetual improvement is made, not just repetition.

An ever-evolving model

Let's say we pull this person out of the model of poor parenting, expose them to the five-step model outlined in this book, and suddenly corrective action begins to take shape. There is a new model, a new example, for that child to follow as they grow their own family. Again, the exponential effect here is nothing short of amazing. Think about all of the future generations, children and grandchildren and their children, who all now have a new, positive, intentional model of parenting to follow.

Here, we no longer have to question decisions of our children because we know they have gone through a model that has brought them to full maturation, and we know that because we've led them through it. We no longer have the right to question our children's decisions. We can safely assume the entire thought process was gone through because the full training process was gone through.

The rest of the results come as a collection of the two parts, two people blending, neither one having more influence over the other. The roles are equal. The relationship has two-way benefits for both parties. Simply put, it's 100-percent mutual.

Practical application

The book you're now holding is the most perfect example of this mutual process playing out and having its full effect. Ron doesn't write. He has never taken a typing class or grown up with technology. If you want him to field-start your tractor with no key or tear apart and repair a tiny carburetor, he's your guy. But he doesn't write. Reid doesn't have kids, at least not when the idea of writing this book started. How could someone who doesn't write author a book? How could someone without any children develop anything worthwhile about parenting? We rely on each other's strengths and skillsets, that's how.

— CHAPTER SIX —

A Never Ending Cycle

Surprising isn't it? With all its complexities and the questions that go along with parenting, there exists a model we can follow with our children that isn't quite as intimidating as we once thought." As parents, we all want the same thing. Ultimately, we want our children to be strong, confident adults who are willing and able to contribute to society in a mighty and powerful way. We want to provide our children every opportunity we had ourselves and more.

It's our belief that if you follow this model and truly put into practice the teachings found in this book, you will have a lasting impact on your children and future generations of your family. This impact not only will benefit them, but it will provide a model for proper parenting that many readers may have missed out on. This new model may very well forever break the chains of bad examples and set your family out on a new trajectory towards happy, healthy relationships and respectful children.

If we're able to commit to establishing discipline early in the lives of our children and follow that up with proper training, we will set a firm foundation on which to build our relationships and our children's future. If we combine that with loving coaching, full of humility, we will have set up a launching pad for our children as they mature and progress into adulthood. If we make a commitment to mentor our children through honest feedback and selfless love, we'll establish a pattern of life-long learning for our children. And if we can eventually progress to a point in which we truly value our children and their spouses as friends, able and ready to contribute to the relationship at new levels, and if we appreciate the unique value and perspectives each of them bring into our lives, we'll have ultimately completed our goal of being successful parents.

This five-stage model is not difficult, but it's not easy. Commit to it, and you won't regret the impact it has for you and your children. Ensure that you take proper time in each step, but progress as quickly as each child is able. Understand that no two kids are the same and each will require a tailored version of this model with their own plan and pace.

Aim ultimately for a successful relationship as adults that benefits both parties equally. And then watch as your children take this new model and continue your legacy of great parenting into future generations.

— ABOUT THE AUTHORS —

Ron Olson

"Jesus bless you."

Ron is the father of five children and the husband of Renee. He raised his five kids on the farm site where he grew up in northeast South Dakota. A third-generation farmer, Ron spent his life working long hours in the field or the shop to feed his family and the community. He was active in various grower groups, at one point serving as a board member of the National Corn Growers Association, and loved being outside on the land and tinkering with equipment projects.

Ron is the youngest of five, and always enjoyed being the life of any party. Rarely was he in a group setting without a smile on his face. An outdoorsman and an animal lover, Ron often brought home and fostered various wildlife he'd encountered while farming. His greatest passion was his relationship with Christ. He loved meeting new people, engaging with friends and strangers alike, sharing the love of Jesus with anyone he encountered.

Ron's life on this Earth came to an abrupt and early end as this book project was nearing conclusion. He ran into the arms of Jesus. It was his desire to share the contents of this book with his own children, grandchildren, and any striving parents.

— ABOUT THE AUTHORS —

Reid Vander Veen

"Make it count."

Reid is the father of three children and lives with his wife, Lauren, on a farm in South Dakota. There the family continues farming traditional crops and also raises aronia berries.

Reid serves on the leadership team at one of the fastest growing churches in America - Embrace Church in Sioux Falls, SD. He's spent his career in sales and marketing, working with organizations ranging from small startups to large global technology firms. An avid outdoorsman, Reid enjoys any opportunity to spend time in or write about the outdoors. He also teaches sales, marketing, and business management courses at the University of Sioux Falls. It's at the same university where Reid obtained both his undergraduate and graduate degrees.

The youngest of two, Reid's childhood memories are made of trips to the campground, riding his bike, fishing at the river, family dinners, and anything a boy could do with a ball in his hand.

Made in USA - Kendallville, IN
85282_9781734412741
11.12.2021 1608